CORFU

TOURIST GUIDE – USEFUL INFORMATION– MAP

GEOGRAPHY - HISTORY - CULTURE AND TRADITION
MONUMENTS - MUSEUMS - ACHILLEION - TOURING THE ISLAND

© 2002 ADAM EDITIONS,KATSIMICHA PEANIA, 190 02 ATTICA
TEL.: 210 6644514-5, FAX. 210 6644512

e-mail: pergamos@adam-editions.gr

C O N T E N T S

THE PHYSIOGNOMY OF CORFU

C orfu lies at the mouth of the Adriatic Sea and faces the shores of the Greek and Albanian mainland, from which it is separated at its northernmost point, St. Stephen's Cape, by a narrow channel only 2 ½ kms. wide. It is the second largest Ionian island (1592 km²) after Cephalonia, and the northernmost island of the group as well as the westernmost point of Greek territory. The island is long and narrow in shape. It becomes narrower towards the south and curves inward towards the coast of Epirus.

It is divided geographically into three parts by two important mountain ranges. The **northern part**, which is the most mountainous, is itself separated into two areas - the *Oros* to the east, including the bulk of Mount Pantocrator, which is the highest peak of the island (906 m.) and *Mt. Gyros* to the west comprising the sheer Vistonas crags and the slightly lower peak of Arakli (506 m.), above Palaiokastritsa. The **middle part**, *"Mesi"*, which is the most important part of the island, is an area of high hills (the highest peak is Aghioi Deka, 579 m.) with small plains in between. This is where the capital of Corfu lies. Finally, the **southern part**, *Lefkimmi*, is mainly a lowland area, with the exception of the wooded Chlomos hill (330 m.).

The largest of the island's plains is near the southwest coast, along Corfu lake, the largest lake, which was formerly a bay, and which acquired its present shape when it was cut off from the sea by a strip of land.

Above:
The Anghelokastro.

Right: Liapades

Corfu's coastline is very varied. The west side is rocky, while the east and north sides are gentler. There are two large bays - Corfu bay and Lefkimmi bay - on the east coast.

A host of small islands surround Corfu - most of them only small clumps of rock around which popular imagination has woven fascinating legends. Thus, the islet of Karavi ("ship") off Kefali point was named after the Phaeacian ship which, having helped Odysseus reach his destination, was turned into stone by Poseidon's wrath; or Pontikonissi, one of the best-known sites in Greece, which is also considered Odysseus' island. In Corfu bay lie two relatively large islands - Vido, which is the ancient Ptychia, and Lazaretto. Most of Corfu is very fertile, the frequent and plentiful rains making for a luxuriant vegetation all the year round, which is one of the island's main characteristics. The olive tree reigns supreme and there are almost four million of them on the island, thanks to the Venetians who were the first to extensively plant and cultivate olive trees here.

Corfu's gentle, Mediterranean climate is characterised by mild winters and cool summers. Humidity levels are high because of the southwesterly and northwesterly winds bringing rain all the year round, except for the three summer months.

Administratively, Corfu, together with the offshore islands of Ereikousa, Othoni and Mathraki to the north, and Paxos and Antipaxos to the south, constitutes a prefecture - one of the most densely-populated in Greece.

LEGEND AND HISTORY

Homer tells us that the first inhabitants of the island were the Phaeacians, who had previously inhabited spacious Hyperia and had settled on the island in the 12th century BC. Their leader was Nausithous, father of Alcinous (*Odyssey*, Book 7). Homer uses the island as the setting of one of the most beautiful episodes of the *Odyssey*, the meeting of Odysseus with Nausicaa, daughter of the Phaeacian king Alcinous and of his wife Arete. Odysseus has been washed ashore, having just escaped Calypso's enchantments, and is welcomed with warmth and generosity in Alcinous' fine palace. Eventually he reveals his identity and relates his ten-year-long adventures. The Phaeacians take Odysseus back on one of their own ships to Ithaca, his homeland, which he has not seen for twenty years.

However, there is also an earlier tradition, which refers to events that occurred before the Trojan War, and which speaks of a foreign settlement on the island prior to Odysseus' visit. This is the legend of the Argonauts, told by the epic poet Apollonius of Rhodes, who lived much later, that is around the 3rd century BC. The Argonauts, having stolen the Golden Fleece from Colchis, and with King Aeetes at their heels, find refuge and a welcome in Alcinous' and Arete's palace. According to this legend, the royal couple intervene to make possible the wedding of Jason and Medea in a safe natural cave near the Hyllaic harbour, after which Medea can no longer return to Colchis. Nor, however, can the Colcheans pursuing the couple, for fear of the anger of king Aeetes, to escape which they settle on the island permanently.

Above: The Doric temple at Kardaki. Late 6th century BC.

Right: Some archaeologists have identified the area of Paleokastritsa with the site of the palace of king Alcinous.

Terracotta figurine. Artemis Kourotrophos from the so-called "Small Sanctuary" at Kanoni. Archaeological Museum of Corfu.

According to the geographer Strabo, the first inhabitants of the island were Liburnians, a seafaring race of Illyrian descent, which held sway over the Dalmatian and Ionian seas. What is certain, in any case, is that Corfu has been inhabited since the Palaeolithic Age (70,000-40,000 BC), as has been proved by archaeological finds - mainly those of the Grava cave at Gardiki, in the northeastern part of the island. At Sidari, on the northern coast of the island, an important Neolithic settlement (6,000-3,000 BC) was found. Life continued here during the Bronze Age (3,000-1,000 BC) as well, when other settlements were founded, mainly on the northwestern coast, at Kefali, Afionas and Ermones.

Ancient times

Towards the middle of the 8th century BC (775-750 BC approximately), the first known Greek settlement on Corcyra was established by the Euboeans

At the end of the 7th century BC, the tyrant Periander was able to impose Corinthian suzerainty on the island. During this period, construction increased markedly and the arts flourished, under the influence of Corinthian artists who came to the island. The circular cenotaph of Menecrates, the temples of Hera and of Artemis, all belong to this period.

After Periander's death, Corcyra regained its independence. This marked the beginning of a period of great economic development for the island, thanks to the growth of its commercial relations with both East and West. Corcyrean products, oil and sweet-scented wine - the famous anthosmias or "flower-scented" wine - were exported in Corcyrean pots known as "Adrian pottery", famous for its solidity, mainly to Epirus and around the Adriatic.

The result of this economic prosperity was that Corcyra could mint its own coins in the 6th century BC and that, in the early 5th century, the building of the famous Corcyrean fleet could begin. During the time of the Persian Wars, Corcyra was the second naval power in the Hellenic world after Athens. On the eve of the naval battle of Salamis, Corcyra had 60 triremes, but she did not finally take part in the conflict, ostensibly because heavy seas prevented her ships from reaching their destination in time.

All these years were years in which Corcyra's civilisation was at its peak. Within fifty years she doubled the size of her fleet, so that on the eve of the Peloponnesian War

(431-404 BC) it numbered 120 ships. Corcyra was thus a naval power to be seriously reckoned with, and one which both the Athenians and the Spartans tried to have on their side.

During the Peloponnesian War, Corcyra initially fought on the side of the Athenians, but soon (427 BC) a terrible civil war broke out in the city, due to the opposition of the oligarchic party to the progressively more democratic form of government of Corcyra, a result of its close relationship with Athens. The internecine struggle between the two political parties (427-425 BC) ended with the victory of the democratic party, but only after the horrible massacre of their opponents, described by Thucydides.

In 410 BC, a second bloody revolt of the oligarchs broke out, ending in the reconciliation of the two parties. Thereafter a policy of neutrality was decided upon regarding Greek political matters, as the oracle of Dodona had also advised. With the application of this policy, Corcyra entered into a new period of peace and prosperity. The democratic party continued to rule Corcyra for many years.

Corcyra's withdrawal from the Second Athenian Alliance after 361 BC, followed by that of other allied cities, contributed to the dissolution of the Alliance, thus paving the way for Macedonian expansion.

In order to counter the Macedonians' expansionist tendencies in Epirus, Corcyra formed an alliance with the Athenians. In 338 BC Corcyra, still an important naval power, fought on the side of the Athenians against Philip II, in the battle of Chaeronia, in which the Macedonians were victorious.

The late 4th century marks the beginning of a series of troubles for once-powerful Corcyra. For approximately a century it becomes the bone of contention between the great powers.

Clay figurine of a seated hare and spherical aryballoi from the Garitsa cemetery. (6th century BC).

Roman times (229 BC-337 AD)

In order to avoid frequent raids and forays, Corcyra placed herself of her own free will under Roman authority. The Romans allowed Corcyra full autonomy and recognised her ancient privileges. In return, Corcyra assumed the obligation to become Rome's ally and to allow her to use the island's ports and navy. As Corcyra was the first stop on the way to the East from Italy, her port was continuously used by the Roman navy and a Roman guard was always stationed there.

During this entire period, Corcyra did not experience any noteworthy military or political events. However she was one of the first Greek cities to convert to Christianity through the teachings, according to tradition, of St. Paul's disciples, Jason and Sosipatros (possible date 48 AD).

During the early years of our era, Corcyra is mentioned in relation to the visits of famous Romans, such as the emperors Nero, Vespasian, Antoninus Pius, Septimius Severus, and the orator Cicero.

Part of the baths belonging to a villa of the Roman period. At Aghios Stephanos, Acharavi.

The Byzantine period (337-1067)

After the death of Theodosius the Great and the division of the Roman Empire into Western and Eastern Empires, Corcyra was included in the Eastern Roman Empire, which later became known as the Byzantine Empire.

During the 5th, 7th and 9th centuries, Corcyra was plagued by barbarian raids of Vandals, Goths and Saracen Arabs, who destroyed many buildings and monuments. The incursion of the Goths, led by Totilas (526 AD), was particularly destructive. The ancient town of Chersoupolis seems to have been gradually abandoned during this period and a new settlement created north of the Canoni peninsula within the small but natural stronghold of

The Byzantine fortress at Gardiki

the double-peaked peninsula. It was then that, for the first time, the Old Fortress was built, forming the nucleus of the new city of Koryfes, as Corfu was called in medieval times.

However, archaeological finds (early Christian basilicas, fortifications, etc.) are proof of a continuous and dynamic local life which flourished after the 8th century, due to the desire of the Byzantines to better ensure free navigation in the Ionian and Adriatic seas.

Corcyra developed into an important trading post both for Byzantium and for its Venetian allies, and this resulted in its impressive economic, demographic and cultural growth. In 876, the Church of Corcyra became a metropolitan church under the authority of the Patriarchate of Constantinople.

In the 11th century, the effort of Byzantium to retain its hold on Corcyra began. As the island constituted the westernmost province of the Empire, it was exposed to the expansionist appetites of the Normans, the Venetians, and other European nations.

In 1199 the island fell into the hands of Venice's rival, Genoa, and in particular of the Genoese pirate, Vetrano Caffaro. The Byzantine Empire had by then fallen into decline, and could no longer protect its more remote territories.

The Venetians (1207-1214)

After the fall of Constantinople into the hands of the Crusaders in the 4th Crusade (1204), the Byzantine state was subjugated and its territories partitioned among the victors. Corcyra was allotted to the Venetians, who had given military assistance to the Crusaders.

Angelokastro, in a rare engraving.

Right: Cassiope, in the northern part of the island, is one of the few fortified positions dating from before the period of Venetian rule. Today the only surviving vestiges are the outer precinct with its strong towers, and the double gate to the east.

The Despotat of Epirus (1214-1267)

Venetian rule was abolished by the Despot of Epirus, Michael I, of the Angelos family, who annexed Corcyra to his despotat, one of the three independent Greek states which had taken the place of the Byzantine Empire after its dissolution by the crusaders (the other two being the Empires of Nicaea and Trebizond). Michael confirmed the privileges which had earlier been given to Corcyra by Byzantine Emperors, and added new ones.

It was during this period that Angelocastron, an extremely strong fortress for its time, was built on one of the precipitous coasts of the island, as a protection against Genoese pirates. These privileges were renewed by Michael II, the successor of Michael I. The annexation of Corcyra to the despotat of Epirus meant better days for the island, but unfortunately this period was only too brief. Despite Michael II's efforts to regain control of the island, Corcyra was finally handed over to the Kingdom of Anjou (1267).

The Angevin rule (1267-1386)

The Angevin occupation lasted for over 100 years and was for Corcyra a period of new troubles and humiliations. The Angevins applied the feudal system while at the same time retaining local laws. The administration of the island was entrusted to a viceroy, the Capitano, who was directly responsible to the king. The island was divided into four bailata or districts: Gyros, Oros, Mesi and Lefkimmi, all ruled by their own bailos. This was when the fortress of Cassiope was built. It did not stand for long, however, as the Venetians demolished it during the first years of their occupation of the island.

In 1294 Charles II ceded Corcyra to his son Philip. ruler of Tarentum, on the occasion of his marriage to Thamar, the lovely daughter of the Epirot despot Nicephorus and Anna Paleologina. Philip became the self-proclaimed ruler (Dominus) of Corcyra and granted many privileges to the islanders. In the meantime, Venice continued to show an unflagging interest in Corcyra.

Thus, in 1386, while the town was being besieged by the forces of the Padovan prince Francis Carrara, and after an agreement according to which the rights and privileges of the inhabitants were guaranteed, the town surrendered of its own free will to the Venetian Admiral of the Adriatic fleet.

The Venetian
belfry of the church
of the Annunciation.

The second period of Venetian rule (1386-1797)

This period is of special importance for the history of Corfu, as the lengthy presence of the Venetians left strong marks on the character of Corfiot life.

The Venetians ruled the island for 400 years. Their main aim in securing its ownership for themselves was to ensure their predominance in trading relations with the East. They were thus particularly interested in fortifying the capital and other important positions in order to defend the island against Turkish attacks.

In contrast to previous occupiers, the Venetians applied policies of religious freedom and of cooperation with the local population. Their attitude towards the Orthodox Church was characterised by understanding and tolerance though, naturally, during these years there was no change in the regime established in the Church by the Angevins.

The Venetians were also interested in agriculture, which of course they adapted to their own needs. They concentrated particularly on developing olive-farming, as the island's climate was particularly favourable to it. The economic benefits of the Venetians from Corfu were important. Her port, through which all the goods from the East passed on their way to Venice, taxation, the rental of public lands, the monopoly on salt etc., all provided constant sources of income.

This period was not peaceful for Corfu. Her vital position in the Adriatic sea and her riches frequently brought foreign forces to her shores.

Gate of the
Venetian village
of Palaia Peritheia.

The Turks tried to seize the island five times (in 1431, 1537, 1571, 1573 1716) - unsuccessfully however, thanks to the constant care of the Venetians to strengthen the fortifications, and to the active and zealous participation of the Corfiots in repelling the enemy.

The enemy assaults resulted in an important decrease in the population, to which Venice responded by bringing over Greeks from the areas that had been lost to the Turks and helping them resettle on the island. Corfu had already, since the 15th century, begun to receive refugees from Constantinople, Epirus and other places that were gradually falling into the hands of the Turks.

In the 16th century these resettlements were more numerous and organised

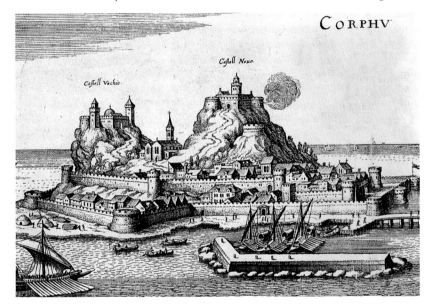

The medieval town before the siege of 1537. Drawing by Weigelin (1580).

and, when Crete was taken in 1669, a large stream of immigrants flowed in. Thus, Corfu's population increased significantly.

In the 17th century Corfu was shaken by serious internal troubles which cost many lives. In 1640, however, a real revolution broke out. The villagers looted the homes of the landowners, forced their way into the town and seized the palace of the Bailos and the Old Fortress gaol, freeing the prisoners. Venice then sent forces and dispersed the rebels. Troubles broke out once more in 1642, and again in 1652, and both uprisings were quenched in blood.

Generally speaking, and despite problems and troubled times, the second period of Venetian rule contributed to the relatively calm and peaceful development of the island, which thus continued, as did the other Venetian possessions, to follow the fortunes of the West, flourishing culturally at a time when the rest of Greece was groaning under the Turkish yoke.

The French republicans (1797-1799)

In 1797 Venice, now in a period of decline, was obliged to accept an alliance with Napoleon, which was tantamount to submission. The Venetian state was abolished. Napoleon, considering the Ionian islands as very important for the success of his politics in the East, sent an army and fleet led by lieutenant-general Gentilly to seize Corfu, in view of its fortified strategic position.

The message of the French Revolution had already come to the island and had inflamed the Corfiots' desire for national independence and for the establishment of a Greek republic on the Ionian islands. Thus, the Corfiots received the French republicans as liberators, seeing in them the end of Venetian rule and of the rule of the nobility. The Venetian emblems and coats of arms were destroyed in the large town square and a tree of freedom symbolically planted on the site of a bonfire where the Libro d'Oro (the "Golden Book" of the nobility) was burnt.

Gentilly formed a provisional town council of 48 members among whom, for the first time, were 10 members of the middle class. Spyridon Theotokis, the head of the republicans, was appointed president.

The possession of the Ionian islands by the French was made formal by the Treaty of Campo Formio and the islands became a French province. During their brief rule, the French founded a Department of Public Education, a public library of 40,000 volumes, and established a printing press on which Rigas Ferraios' "Thourios" (revolutionary song) was republished. Despite this, French rule was considered worse than that of the Venetians.

The Turko-Russian occupation and the Septinsular State (1799-1807)

Napoleon's expansionist policies worried Russia, who proposed an alliance to Turkey. The Turko-Russian fleet arrived in Corfu and began to besiege the island. The French, despite their internal problems. Fighting went on for four months and it was only when the Turko-Russian fleet had managed to neutralise the defence of the little island of Vido, which constituted a natural bastion, that the French decided to sue for a truce. The island was surrendered to the leaders of the allied fleet, admirals Uchakov and Abdel-Kadir-Bey. In Corfu the nobility was immediately restored to power.

With the treaty of Constantinople in 1800, signed by Russia, Turkey and Great Britain, the establishment of the Septinsular State as a single autonomous state was formalised and the new constitution approved. The state assumed the obligation to pay taxes to Turkey.

When the Turko-Russian war broke out, the Septinsular state found itself on Russia's side. By the Treaty of Tilsit in 1807 between the Russians

and Napoleon, the Seven Islands were handed over to the French for the second time.

The Imperial French (1807-1814)

When they took over the Ionian islands, the French abolished the Septinsular or Heptanesian Republic, and declared the islands French provinces. The islanders thus became French citizens.

The second French period was one which left good memories as, this time, the French showed a greater interest in Corfu. They turned their attention to agriculture, introducing new cultures (potatoes, tomatoes, etc.), to the advancement of education - the Ionian Academy was founded in 1808 - to the organisation and functioning of public services and, finally, to architecture and town-planning, which owes much to French good taste.

In the meantime, the British, who were unhappy with the French occupation of the Ionian islands began, in 1809, to occupy Corfu's neighbouring islands. After taking Paxos, they blockaded Corfu closely. The island would not have fallen into their hands, as the French garrison was very strong, but when Napoleon fell, in 1814, the French were finally forced to give it up.

The wooden bridge and the entrance to the Old Fortress towards the middle of the 19th century.

The British Protectorate (1814-1864)

Thus, despite the withdrawal of the French, the desire of the Corfiots for national independence was not yet to be fulfilled. Unfortunately, at the Congress of Vienna in 1815, the proposal by John Capodistrias, the Russian plenipotentiary (and himself a Corfiot), that independence be granted to the Ionian islands, was not accepted by the other powers (Great Britain, Austria and Prussia). However, thanks to his efforts and his authority, Capodistrias was able to prevent the British from gaining full control of the Seven Islands. Thus, by the Treaty of Paris (1815), the "United States of the Ionian Islands" as they were then called, were recognised as a free and independent state, albeit under the direct and exclusive protection of Great Britain. They were to be governed by a British Lord High Commissioner, whose seat would be in Corfu.

However, the period of the British Protectorate in Corfu had several positive aspects. The Church was practically allowed full freedom, and it was then that, for the first time, Greek was established as the official language. Corfu owes to the British its dense network of roads, still in use today, as well as the construction of a fine aqueduct, supplying Corfu town with water. The British also organised education at all levels and, in 1824, thanks to the generosity of Frederick North, 5th Earl of Guilford, a new

The statue of Ioannis Capodistrias on the Esplanade

The new Theatre of Corfu was built in 1893 to replace the San Giacomo.

The library of the town of Corfu. A characteristic building of the last century.

Ionian Academy was founded, which is considered to be the first Greek university. The town was also adorned with beautiful new public buildings.

Incorporation of Corfu into the Greek state (1864)

The opportunity for Corfu's union with Greece was provided when the new king of Greece was chosen. Britain ceded the Ionian islands to Greece in exchange for the choice of the Danish prince, William, a man enjoying Britain's trust, as George I, King of Greece. The conditions accompanying the cession required that the Ionian islands remain permanently neutral and demolish their fortifications. Thanks to the efforts of the Greek Government, however, a new treaty was signed between the Great Powers and Greece, according to which only Corfu and Paxos were required to remain neutral. Thus, on the 21st of May 1864, the union of the Ionian islands with Greece at last became a reality, and was welcomed with enthusiasm both in Corfu and in Athens.

During World War I, in contravention of this neutrality, Corfu was used as an allied base by the British, French and Italian armies, and as a base for the reorganisation of the Serbian army after its defeat (late 1916).

Corfu was bombed again by the Italians in 1940, during the Greco-Italian war, and the town was badly damaged once more when it was taken over by the Germans in 1943. Many important buildings were destroyed at that time, such as the Library, the Ionian Parliament building, the theatre and many churches.

→

The Old town of Corfu.

LETTERS AND ARTS 17ᵗʰ-19ᵗʰ CENTURIES

The cultural elements brought to Corfu by refugees fleeing their enslaved homelands, combined with local traditions, the particular geographic position the island occupies, which made it a link between East and West, its history and political situation (control by a succession of foreign conquerors), all were basic factors contributing to Corfu's cultural renaissance in the 18th century and to its becoming, in the 19th century, the cultural centre of the whole of Greece.

Thus, in the 17th century (1656), the first literary seminary was founded, the Accademia Degli Assicurati (Academy of the Secured) followed shortly afterwards by the Accademia Dei Fertili. However, the cultural development of the Corfiots was soon checked by the great Turkish invasion in 1716, which brought about a general decline in the life of the island. In 1732 the Academy of the Errants ("Quos Phoebus Vocat Errantes") was founded, but neither of these three educational institutions was actually very effective. The eminent Corfiot church-men, Evgenios Voulgaris and Nikiphoros Theotokis, held a special place among the learned citizens of the time, and are numbered among the "Teachers of the Nation". They endeavoured to preserve Greek tradition while fully aware, at the same time, of the West's contribution to the body of scientific knowledge. They used Greek as the language for their writings at a time when the Corfiots - at least the urban Corfiots - spoke and wrote in Italian, since most of them had studied in Italy.

In 1797 the Republican French set up the first printing press on Corfu, which made it possible to publish newspapers and magazines in Italian and French. During the second period of French rule, in 1808, the Ionian Academy was

Above: Detail from the painting "Corfu Landscape", by Charalambos Pachis (1873).

Left: Traditional dress of Corfu. Postcard printed in Corfu.

founded, on the active initiative of John Capodistrias among others. In 1815, Pavlos Prosalentis, a pupil of Canova, founded the first school of Fine Arts. In 1817, Greek became recognised as the official language, though this decision was only applied in practice in 1851, and efforts were made to promote it by the publication of books in Greek.

An event of great importance was the establishment in 1824, for the second time, of the Ionian Academy - considered to be the first Greek university - by Frederick North, 5th Earl of Guilford, who was Director of Public Education in the Ionian Islands and an ardent Philhellene and admirer of ancient Greek civilisation. It was in the Academy that the Greek language was officially established for the first time. For forty years (1824-1864) the Academy, whose symbol was the owl, provided learning through its four faculties (theology, literature, law and medicine). Several noted personalities of the time taught there, such as the poet Andreas Calvos, the philosopher and president of the Ionian Parliament, Petros Armenis, and others. Corfu's cultural and intellectual life reached its peak when the great national poet of Greece, Dionysios Solomos, came to settle on the island. Solomos lived in Corfu from 1828 to the time of his death in 1857. He fervently supported the idea of the Ionian islands' union with Greece and applied all his efforts to making it a reality.

When he came to settle in Corfu, he gathered around him a literary group which also cultivated the living demotic language, in contrast to the attitude prevailing in Athens at the time, which favoured an archaic form of Greek. This group of writers made up the well-known Corfu Literary School, which counted among its representatives Iakovos Polylas, Gerasimos Marcoras, G. Calosgouros and the followers of Solomos' tradition, Nikolaos Koyevinas, Stefanos Chrysomallis and Lorenzos Mavilis.

Portrait of the national poet, Dionysios Solomos, who lived in Corfu until his death in 1857.

MUSIC

Corfu was also an important musical centre. The Corfiots' love of music is evident in their every expression-even in the characteristic lilt of their speech. In 1840, on the initiative of the composer Nikolaos Mantzaros, the Old Philharmonic Society was founded and became the musical nursery of Greece. Mantzaros also set to music part of a long poem by Dionysios Solomos, the Hymn to Liberty, which became the Greek National Anthem in 1864. In 1890, a new Philharmonic Society was founded, known as the Mantzaros Philharmonic. Other well known Corfiot composers are Xyndas, who composed the operetta «The Candidate», Samaras, and others.

"May Day in Corfu". Charalambos Pachis. National Gallery Collection.

Stephanos
Tzangarolas:
St. Alexius,
"The man of God".
Church of the
Antivouniotissa
(late 17th century).

PAINTING

After the final occupation of Crete by the Turks in 1669, many Cretan icon painters, bearers of the Cretan post-Byzantine tradition - which incorporated strong Western elements - settled permanently or temporarily, on their way to the West, in the Ionian Islands . They found fertile ground for their creativity, and helped decorate churches which were being built in large numbers in the 16th and 17th centuries, thanks to the religious freedom granted by the Venetians and to the prevailing material and cultural prosperity. The style of painting of these artists is characterised by the adoption of humanistic elements of the western Renaissance, which softens the austerity and transcendental spirituality of the purely Byzantine aesthetic style. One of the most famous of these icon painters was Michael Damaskinos, who worked in Corfu for a few years during this period and who paved the way for the introduction of Cretan painting in the Ionian islands at the end of the 16th century.

The **Heptanesian School** developed with Corfu and Zakynthos as its centre. The religious painters belonging to this School adapted their art to the pictorial and morphological precepts of the Western art of their time. The work of the great Italian artists of the 16th century, such as Veronese, and of the 17th and 18th centuries served as models for the Heptanesian painters who, for the most part, had studied in Italy.

Panayiotis Doxaras (1662-1729) who, with his theoretical treatise "Peri Zographias" ("On Painting"), appears as the first advocate in Greece of the naturalistic principles and techniques of western European art, had studied in Rome and in Venice and admired the Venetian painters Tintoretto, Titian

and Veronese. He worked in Corfu and founded a school in the Ionian Islands which attracted many followers. Doxaras consciously incorporated elements that differed much from Byzantine tradition. In the 17th and 18th centuries, the artists Theodoros Poulakis, the Tzanes brothers, Stephanos Tzangarolas and others, all worked in Corfu.

In the early 19th century, the sculptor Pavlos Prosalentis (1784-1837) founded his own School of Fine Arts. This School was succeeded by the Fine Arts section of the Ionian Academy in 1808 and later, in 1815, a third school was founded, with Prosalentis as its director.

This was the Public Academy of Fine Arts, where architecture, sculpture and painting were taught. Besides Prosalentis himself, the painter Gerasimos Pitzimanos, Prosalentis' pupil Dionysios Veyias and the architect John Chronis all taught here.

During the 19th century the Ionian Islands produced a series of noteworthy painters who, however, did not manage to revive the local artistic tradition.

Icon by Michael Damaskinos: SS. Justine, Serge and Bacchus. Church of the Antivouniotissa (painted after 1571).

THE ANCIENT CITY

I n the 8th century BC, the Corinthian colony of Chersoupolis was founded on the east coast, much further south than the centre of the modern town, on the site later called Palaeopolis. Its original position was on the neck of the Canoni peninsula, between the two ancient harbours, the Hyllaic harbour to the west, which corresponds to the Halikiopoulos lagoon today, and the harbour of Alcinous to the northeast, which faced the mainland of Epirus and corresponds to the filled-up area of Anemomylos today. The town gradually spread south to the Figaretto area of today. In the classical period, the town reappears, with well-defined limits and a town-planning system. It was walled on three sides. The north wall (probably of the 5th century BC) protected the town from the north.

A tower, known as the Nerantzihas tower, still standing near the cemetery today, is the only remaining part of this wall. It was spared from destruction because a Byzantine church, the Church of Our Lady, was housed inside it. The wall on the coastward side (also of the 5th century BC) protected the vulnerable eastern shore of the Canoni peninsula, while two towers defended the entrance to the harbour of Alcinous. The lower part of the eastern tower in the port became the base of the church of St. Athanasios in the Anemomylos area. Finally, the south wall (4th century BC) isolated the town from the tip of the peninsula.

The acropolis stood on the highest point of the Canoni hills in the Analypsis area of today, and the agora was in Palaeopolis, opposite what is today the entrance to the villa of Mon Repos. Shrines, public buildings, baths, workshops, all stood here, though only a few traces of these remain. They were destroyed in the early Christian era (5th century AD) by Bishop Jovian in order to make place for the splendid five-aisled basilica of Palaeopolis. The residential area was situated on the western side of the Canoni peninsula.

Above: The Hyllaic harbour of the ancient town in an old tinted postcard.

Left:Detail of the decoration of the bronze hydria. A Dionysiac scene. A young satyr supports a naked, bearded, inebriated man.

The burial ground of the Archaic and Classical age was outside the north wall, in the present-day Garitsa area. Here, various graves were excavated, and there must have been rich funerary monuments, such as that of Menecrates, which was discovered in 1843 during the execution of road works. It is a round cenotaph, made of limestone blocks, and has a conical roof. The Tomb of Menecrates dates back to approximately 600 BC. The shrines were situated in various places. In the ancient agora, in the two ancient harbours, in the southern part of the ancient town and in the acropolis area.

The circular cenotaph of menecrates, at Garitsa

The first shrines were open-air shrines. At the end of the 7th and the early 6th centuries BC, magnificent temples were built, such as those of Hera and of Artemis. The temple of Hera, the largest and most important temple on the island, was situated on the acropolis (Mon Repos grounds). No part of the original temple was discovered on the site, but its position was located, and numerous architectural remains and votive offerings were uncovered nearby. It appears to have been destroyed during the civil wars, most probably at the end of the 5th century BC, and was built again around 400 BC.

The temple of Artemis, was situated close to the Hyllaic harbour by the NW gate of the city, in the Aghioi Theodoroi area of today and very near the monastery of the same name. It was built in the early 6th century BC (590-580 BC) of limestone, and its roof was initially covered with terracotta roof fittings. This was replaced by marble in 530 BC. Scant remains of this tem-

The bases of the columns of the temple of Artemis, in the area of Aghioi Theodoroi (585 BC).

The remains of the Kardaki temple at Mon Repos, the harbour of Alcinous and, in the background, the Old Fortress, as depicted in an old engraving.

ple can be seen, among which its impressive altar, 25 m in length, which is decorated with triglyphs and unadorned metopes. The most important find is the west pediment of the temple, decorated with a monumental sculptural group, dominated by a Gorgon - a unique example of early Archaic art. At the end of the 6th and the 5th centuries, other smaller temples were built. On the Mon Repos grounds, the temple of Kardaki was discovered by chance in 1822 by the British, when they began to dig in order to find out why the Kardaki spring had suddenly run dry. The reason, they discovered, was that a portion of the temple, which until then had been hidden, had subsided and was blocking the channel through which the water flowed. The Kardaki temple dates from the 6th century BC. It was a Doric temple with 11 columns on its long sides and 6 on its narrow sides. Despite the fact that its east side, to seaward, slid down and was lost, it is the best-preserved temple on Corfu. It is said to have been dedicated to Apollo, though this is not absolutely certain, and it seems that this is where the annual commemorative festival of Jason's wedding to Medea took place, during which offerings were brought to the Nymphs, the Nereids and Apollo.

The temple of Dionysus was situated in the southern part of the town, in the Figaretto quarter of today. From this temple comes the left section of a late Archaic pediment in poros stone. It depicts a Dionysiac banquet and dates from approximately 500 BC. Other temples of the 5th century BC are those of the Pythian Apollo, whose altar and cella were found close to the temple of Artemis, and the small open-air shrine of Apollo the Corcyrean, with its oblong grid and courtyard, which was found close to the temple of Hera.

MONUMENTS OF THE EARLY- CHRISTIAN AND BYZANTINE PERIOD

In important early Christian building in Corfu is the Palaeopolis basilica, also known as Aghia Kerkyra. It is near the entrance to Mon Repos, where the centre of the ancient town used to be.

This 5th-century church was one of the most magnificent basilicas of the time. It had five aisles and two narthexes and was richly decorated with sculptures and mosaic floors. Pre-existing building materials were used for its construction, as attested by the inscription on the lintel of the western entrance. According to this inscription, written in hexametric form, Jovian, Bishop of Corcyra in the 5th century, built this church after destroying the pagan altars. The buildings, which occupied the site before the basilica was built and whose materials contributed to its construction, were mainly a Doric temple of the 5th century BC and a Roman Odeum.

According to popular tradition, the church was dedicated to the daughter of King Cercillinus, Kerkyra, who was converted to Christianity and suffered martyrdom. This basilica was destroyed during the 6th century raids and in its place was erected a smaller three-aisled basilica which was also destroyed in the 11th century.

A still smaller church was built in the 12th century, was restored in 1537,

The ruins of the basilica of Palaeopolis which, according to tradition, was erected by Bishop Jovian, in the 5th century AD, in honour of St. Kerkyra.

and was finally severely damaged by bombs during World War II. The visitor today can see nothing but ruins. The church has no roof and its apse is gone. Parts of the mosaic floor can still be seen, however, as well as some architectural fragments, in the Christian Art collection housed in the Royal Palace.

Around the middle of the 6th century, the ancient town was destroyed by Goth raids and its inhabitants forced to take refuge in the little peninsula of the Old Fortress, which was easier to defend. Here the new town centre gradually developed. The only fresco which can still be seen is that which depicts St. Arsenios, a 10th-century bishop. This fresco dates from the 11th century. A large part of the iconographic decoration of the church was executed by the famous Cretan artist Emmanuel Tzanes Bounialis, who worked in Corfu at the end of the 16th century. The icons of the two saints, to whom the church is dedicated, have been attributed to him. Tzanes also painted the icon of St. Cyril, patriarch of Alexandria, which has been taken to the Museum, while icons of St. John Damascene and of St. Gregory Palamas are still in situ. In the churchyard is the tomb of Catherine, wife of the last despot of Mystras, Thomas Palaeologos, who died here in 1462.

The church of SS. Jason and Sosipater at Garitsa. It is dated to about 1000 AD.

THE TOWN OF CORFU

T he old town of Corfu is very much worth wandering about in, not only because of its important historical landmarks but also because of its unique character. The flagstone streets, the tall buildings and the volta at the Liston, the picturesque kantounia and the lovely old churches, the mourayia (sea walls), the contrafossa dividing the Old Fortress from the Esplanade, give visitors the impression that they are strolling in some corner of Venice. Among the loveliest walks is that around the vast **Esplanade**. Three historical periods coexist within it: the Venetian period, represented by the *Old Fortress*, the French period by the volta at the Liston, and the British Protectorate, of which the *Palace* is a fitting reminder. The view of the **contrafossa** through the Municipal Gardens is very picturesque.

The Old Fortress. The Contrafossa, the moat built to separate the Old Fortress from the outer city, the Xopolis.

Old Fortress

The Old Fortress dominates the Spianada, and is linked to the town by a fixed iron bridge, 60 m in length. This bridge, which spans the moat, or contrafossa, used to be wooden and was drawn up at night to isolate the citadel for greater safety. The Byzantines were the first to fortify one of the two peaks of the citadel, which became known in Venetian times as "Castel Vecchio" or "Castel a Mare". The Venetians later fortified the other peak as well, and built bastions, winding galleries and tunnels. They also completed the military installations of the Fortress by adding new barracks, prisons and granaries, and erecting buildings to house the military and political authorities and members of the aristocracy.

Today, the Venetian walls, as well as the additional fortifications built by the British, can still be seen in the Old Fortress. Most of the surviving buildings, however, date from the period of British rule and are those that served as accommodation for the military authorities and as barracks for the garrison. The church of St. George stands out among these buildings, as does the great clock tower. The church was built by the British in 1840 in Doric style, on the southern side of the Fortress. The entire area of the Old Fortress is very picturesque and it is worth climbing to the top of the cliff, to enjoy one of the most beautiful views of the town.

In front of the entrance to the bridge leading to the Old Fortress stands the statue of field marshal von der Schulenburg, erected by the Venetians during the field marshal's lifetime as a token of gratitude for his services during the last great siege by the Turks in 1716.

The Palace of St. Michael and St. George

The Palace of St. Michael and St. George, which stands along the northern side of the Esplanade, constitutes one of the finest buildings in Corfu and one of its most impressive landmarks. Built in Georgian style, it is the grandest building of the British period and unique in the entire Mediterranean. Its construction began in 1819 and it served as the residence of the British High Commissioners.

It was also the seat of the Order of St. Michael and George. This Order was instituted in 1818 to honour British colonial officials serving in the Ionian islands. In the period between 1864 and 1913 the palace became the summer residence of the Greek royal family. It is built entirely in Maltese stone after plans by Sir George Whitmore, a British colonel of the Royal Engineers. A Doric colonnade adorns its façade and its two entrances, on the side towards the Esplanade, have triumphal arches on which the names of the saints of the Order are inscribed. On the top of the building, reliefs allegorically represent the Ionian islands: Pegasus with Bellerophon stands for Levkas, the head of Odysseus for Ithaca, the mythical heroes Cephalos and Zakynthos for Cephalonia and Zakynthos respectively, a trident for Paxos, and Aphrodite with a dolphin for Cythera. Corfu is represented by an ancient ship. All are works by the Corfiot sculptor Prosalentis. In the magnificent staterooms of the Palace (throne room, ballroom and dining room) adorned with beautiful marble fireplaces and crystal chandeliers and decorated with monograms and the insignia of the Order of St. Michael and St. George, medals were awarded with pomp and circumstance during British rule, and other important ceremonies took place. Small gardens, beautifully laid out, surround the building. In the small garden in the centre stands the statue of the British High Commissioner, Sir Frederick Adam, also by Pavlos Prosalentis.

The palace of St. Michael and St. George

Left: During the second period of French rule (1807-1814), the Spianada was converted into a tree-lined square. Its western side was bordered by the huge building complex of the Liston, ornamented, at ground level, by an impressive arched portico.

The Town Hall

Barely 100 m away from the centre of the Esplanade, in Evgeniou Voulgari street, stands an elegant old building, reminiscent of the Venetian period. This building, which is today the Town Hall, was once the Loggia Nobilei. It was built in stages between 1661 and 1693, to serve as a club for the officers of the Venetian fleet, and was used, during the same period, as a meeting place or loggia for members of the aristocracy. It is built of Siniès stone in Renaissance style and is the only building with dressed stone in town. Its façades are adorned with beautiful carvings and on its eastern wall is a bust of the Venetian admiral, and later doge, Francesco Morosini. The four children's figures around him symbolise his virtues.

In the mid-18th century (1720) the building was converted into a theatre, named San Giacomo from the nearby Roman Catholic cathedral of St. James built in 1632. This building is closely linked to the history of the theatre in Greece, and particularly in the Ionian islands, and contributed greatly to the theatrical fame of Corfu. In 1733 it also became the stage for the performance of operas and lyric plays. In the early years of the 20th century a new theatre was built in Corfu town, but this was destroyed in 1943 and the Loggia, with an extra floor added on, became the Town Hall.

The Maitland Rotunda

This is another landmark of the period of the British Protectorate. It stands on the NE side of the Esplanade. It is a circular building with Ionian columns and was erected in honour of the British High Commissioner, Sir Thomas Maitland, in 1816.

Prefecture

Another fine building, also dating from the period of British rule and designed by the architect Chronis, is the Prefecture, which stands at the top end of the Esplanade. It was bought by the Government of the Ionian State to serve as the residence of the President of the Ionian Senate.

The Reading Society

The building housing the Reading Society of Corfu, on the west side of the northern section of the Esplanade, is another interesting building of the period. The Reading Society was founded in 1836, for the intellectual enrichment and enjoyment of its members. It contains an important library specialising in books on the Ionian islands, and collections of paintings and icons.

Ionian Parliament

The Ionian Parliament, also a building of the period of British rule, designed by the Corfiot architect I. Chronis (1855), stands at the end of Moustoxydi street (Platy Kantouni). It is historically important, since this is where the last Ionian Parliament, on the 23rd of September 1863, voted for the union of the Ionian Islands with Greece. The building has been restored and houses the Museum of the Fighters for Heptanesian Independence.

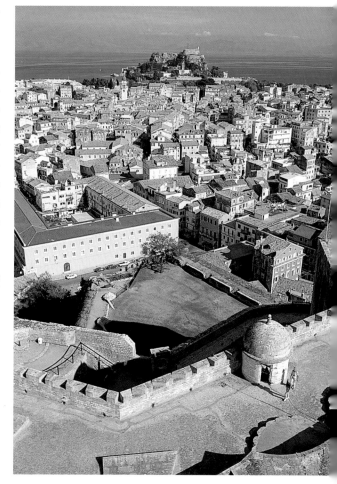

In the *Anthon*, the flower garden of the **Municipal Gardens**, stands the statue of Lord Guilford. This is a marble statue by the sculptor C. Aperghis and shows the founder of the Ionian Academy in his academic robes, holding an open book in his hand. Nearby are the busts of two famous Corfiots, the poet Lorenzos Mavilis and the writer Dinos Theotokis.

As one's gaze leaves the Esplanade, after lingering on the Palace, it embraces a magnificent view towards the coastal road with its sea walls. Along this road and up to the Cathedral, the narrow lanes lead to the **Campiello**, the oldest quarter of the town, where the oldest houses and many historic churches of Corfu are to be found.

Another notable landmark of the old town is the **central market**. Nikiphorou Theotoki is the most interesting street here, as the rows upon rows of volta resting on their stone columns, and the tall buildings, present one of the most characteristic aspects of the Old Town.

The New Fortress

The New Fortress, also known as the *Fortress of San Marco,* was built by the Venetians in 1576, shortly after the second Turkish siege. It was here that the wall protecting the town on the west side ended. At the foot of the fortress nestles the old harbour.

The French, and later the British, completed the fortifications and the buildings of the fortress. Its two beautiful gates are especially interesting. They have survived, almost untouched, to our day, and bear the emblem of the Most Serene Republic, the winged Lion of St. Mark.

The Douglas Obelisk

Standing at the junction of the Garitsa coastal road and Alexandras Avenue, this landmark, also belonging to the same period, was erected in honour of the Lord High Commissioner, Sir Howard Douglas, to whom Corfu owes various public works and charitable institutions.

On one of the sides of the pedestal, an inscription in ancient Greek records the High Commissioner's good works while, on the other three sides, Douglas' coat of arms and views of Corfu are carved in relief.

The northeastern gate of the Old Fortress,

Below:
The marble obelisk, known as the "Douglas

CHURCHES

The churches within the town do not face in any particular direction, as space is so limited and they are usually squeezed in between houses.

St. Spyridon's

St. Spyridon's is the most famous church on Corfu. It was built in 1590 and replaced an older church which stood in the Sarocco quarter and was demolished so that the town walls could be erected.

It is a single-nave basilica, as are most of Corfu's churches. Its exterior decoration is not particularly interesting, apart from the elegant and impressive clock belfry which resembles that of its almost contemporary Greek church of St. George in Venice. Icons and ceiling frames grace the church's interior. The painting of the ceiling was completed in 1727 and was the work of Panayiotis Doxaras - it was considered his masterpiece.

Below: The procession of the celebration of St. Spyridon's feast day.

Right: The belfry of the church of St. Spyridon

The icons were replaced in the 19th century by copies by Nicholas Aspiotis, but these are far inferior to the originals. The four icons of the narthex are noteworthy and were painted by the Corfiot S. Sperantzas. The iconostasis of the church, made of Carrara and Paros marble, is a work by the Austrian architect M. Mauers (1864). A silver casket, made in Vienna in the 19th century, contains the embalmed body of the Saint. St. Spyridon, who is the patron saint of Corfu, was a Cypriot bishop who took part in the

First Ecumenical Synod of Nicaea (325). His remains were kept in Constantinople and were brought to Corfu after the fall of the city, together with the relics of St. Theodora, which are now kept in the Cathedral. Corfu celebrates St. Spyridon's feast day on the 12th of September, but it also celebrates the days on which the embalmed body of the Saint is carried in solemn procession through the streets of the town. These processions were established during the period of Venetian rule and are still held every year in commemoration of miracles performed by St. Spyridon on various occasions in the history of the island.

The Cathedral of Panaghia Speliotissa. This church, together with that of St. Spyridon, is the most important in the town of Corfu. It is a three-aisled basilica, built in 1577, on the site of a previous church dedicated to St. Vlasios (Blaise).

The cathedral of the Virgin Speliotissa.

It owes its name to the fact that the icon of the Virgin was brought here from an old church which had stood on the small square of the New Fortress and which was demolished by the British in order to open a new entrance to the Fort.

The iconostasis is a fine work of art in the Byzantine style. The church celebrates its feast-day on the 15th of August, day of the Dormition of the Virgin, and also on the 11th of February, day of the holy martyr St. Vlasios and of St. Theodora, whose relics are kept here.

Aghios Nikolaos ton Gerondon. This church was built in the 16th century and is one of the oldest and most important churches in Corfu town. It stands in the Campiello quarter and used to be the Cathedral of the Great Protopapas. Restoration work has significantly altered the appearance of the exterior of the church.

Panaghia Antivouniotissa. This church is also in the Campiello quarter and was probably built in the 15th century. Its name does not refer to the Virgin Mary but to the church's position, opposite the Ovriovouni mountain. This church used to be one of the richest in town.

Panaghia Kremasti. This is one of Corfu's most beautiful churches and is also known as Panaghia Kecharitomeni (Our Lady Full of Grace). Built in the 16th century as a single-nave basilica, it appears to have had an exterior narthex on three of its sides, of which only the west side has survived.

Church of Christ Pantocrator. This 16th-century church has recently been restored, since it suffered serious damage during the 1943 bombings. Its iconostasis, painted by Georgios Chry-soloras (18th century) is particularly interesting, while paintings by Em. Tzanes from an old 17th-century iconostasis have also survived.

Aghios Ioannis o Prodromos. This 16th-century church is a single-nave basilica, with a spacious narthex which served as a burial ground, on its north, south and west sides. For many years it was used by the Great Protopapas as a cathedral. It has a simple iconostasis made of Siniès marble.

Panaghia ton Xenon. This church is a basilica with a central nave separated from the two side aisles by two rows of marble columns. It is exceedingly rich in icons, liturgical vessels and silverwork. It owes its lavish decoration to the Greeks from Epirus, to whom it belonged, and who had fled to Corfu during the Ottoman occupation bringing with them the treasures from their own churches. The ceiling is painted by N. Koutouzis (18th century) and there are two beautiful icons by Tzanes, depicting the Virgin Enthroned and St. Anthony.

Emmanuel Tzanes:
St. Cyril, patriarch
of Alexandria, 1654.
Antivouniotissa
Museum.

The monastery Our Lady of Tenedos. The latter was built just outside the walls of the New Fortress and is the most genuinely baroque building of the island. It owes its name to the refugee Cap-uchin monks who, fleeing from the Turks on the island of Tenedos, had found a haven in Corfu. In this church was housed the first Greek printing press during the time of the Septinsular State.

In the Mandouki area stands the monastery of **Our Lady Platytera** (18th century), which was destroyed by bombs in 1799 during the conflicts between the Russians, Turks and French, but was immediately rebuilt. In this church are buried John Capodistrias, first president of Greece, the Corfiot historian Andreas Moustoxydis, and the hero of the War of Independence, Photos Tzavellas.

MUSEUMS

T he **Archaeological Museum** he Archaeological Museum is housed in a building inaugurated about ten years ago and situated in Vraila street, a few minutes away from the Garitsa coastal road. This is where all the archaeological finds brought to light on the island are kept. The most important exhibit of the Museum is the west pediment of the temple of Artemis - the famous Gorgon pediment, contemporary with the temple itself (590 BC). This is the most ancient surviving pediment in Greece and one of the most important surviving groups of the monumental sculpture of the Archaic period to have been discovered to date.

This huge sculptural group is made of poros stone (22.50 m in width, 4.50 m in height). The central motif is dominated by the Gorgon between her sons Pegasus and Chrysaor (to her right and left respectively as seen by the viewer). According to mythology, the Gorgon, or Medusa, was beheaded by Perseus, who had to perform this deed without looking at her as he would otherwise be turned to stone. From her blood were born her two sons, Pegasus and Chrysaor. The monstrous Gorgon, girded by snakes, is seen running to the right, with bent knees, in accordance with the conventions of Archaic art, but with her torso and head facing the viewer. Pegasus, who was the emblem of Corinth and whose figure has been almost entirely lost, was shown with his front legs on the Gorgon's arm, while Chrysaor was holding a sword, which has not been found. On his face is one of the most beautiful "Archaic smiles" of early Archaic art. This central composition is framed by a pair of wild animals - two great mythical creatures with the bodies of panthers and the heads of lions - the marks of their fur indicated by groups of concentric circles. Their heads are turned towards the viewer. Only the head of the ani-

Above: The Gorgon pediment from the large temple of Artemis, in the Aghioi Theodoroi area.

**Left:
The young Zeus, brandishing his thunderbolt, overcomes the kneeling Titan, Iapetus. Detail from the Gorgon pediment (585-580 BC).**

Chrysaor,
one of the
Gorgon's sons
and the Gorgon's
serpentine girdle .

mal on the right has survived. In the two corners of the pediment the composition is complemented by scenes from the Battle of the Olympians and the Titans or Giants, which resulted in the overthrow of the ancient deities by the Olympian gods.

The presence of the Gorgon in the central area of the pediment is somewhat strange, however. The wild beasts on either side lend her the attributes of a great Nature goddess, attributes which, however, have survived from prehistoric religions as belonging to Artemis. In the same room there are also various fragments of the same temple or of smaller buildings pertaining to the same shrine. Another pediment worthy of interest was found in the Figaretto quarter of Canoni. It is the left part of an Archaic pediment dating from approximately 500 BC and depicting a Dionysiac symposium or drinking party. Also particularly interesting are the prehistoric finds, such as pieces of pottery of the early Neolithic age from Sidari (6th millennium BC), pyrite stones, tools and vessels of the Bronze Age. One of the most beautiful exhibits of the Museum is the Archaic lion found close to the tomb of Menecrates.

In the Museum are also housed the finds of the excavations on the Mon Repos estate. Architectural elements from the temple of Hera - in particular the impressive antefixes in the shape of lions' heads, of a woman's face, of a gorgon, and a disc-shaped antefix with a painted rosette (late 7th century BC) - a small bronze statue of a young man from a Laconian workshop, which probably decorated the rim of a cauldron (6th century BC), the small head of a kouros (530 BC), a small Corinthian bronze horse (late 8th century BC) - one of the oldest offerings in the sanctuary - and a terracotta quadriga with its charioteer, draw

**The Lion of
Menecrates
(late 7th cent. BC).**

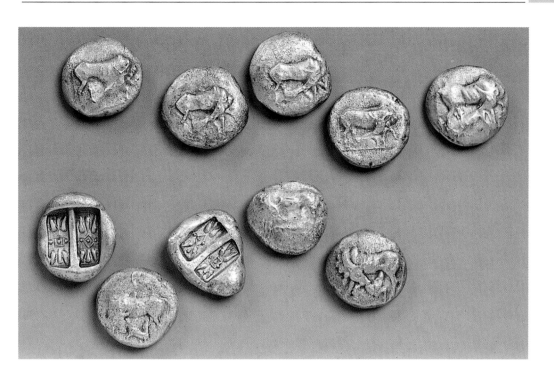

the visitor's attention. Noteworthy, too, are the finds from the temple of Apollo and particularly three spearheads, one of them of bronze with an inscription showing that it was made especially to be offered to the god, and a lead tablet on whose two sides are inscribed the temple's yearly revenues.

Silver Corcyrean coins.

From the excavations of the small shrine of Artemis at Canoni one can see some of the terracotta statuettes found in large numbers and most of which represent the goddess with a bow and a deer (approximately 480 BC).

Attic black-figure "louterion" from the Garitsa cemetery.

There are also two showcases with coins found on Corfu. The silver coin showing a cow nuzling her calf is the one minted in Corcyra when the island obtained its independence from Corinth. The visitor to the Museum can also see Corinthian pottery and Corcyrean imitations (7th-6th cent. BC), many of which came from the Garitsa graves, lead tablets with inscriptions recording debts (late 6th - early 5th century BC), bronze statues of the 5th century BC, Laconian and black-figure pots, and also a large number of funerary stelae and Archaic inscriptions.

Lastly, also interesting is the room containing exhibits from the 4th century BC to Roman times. Most of these are sculptures standing on bases.

Museum of Asiatic Art

The Museum of Asiatic Art is housed in the Palace of St. Michael and St. George which, as we have seen, was built between 1819 and 1824.

The palace is composed of a three- storeyed central building on the three sides of a rectangle. Two ground floor wings are joined to the main building by two arches and a colonnade of thirty-two columns. On the ground floor, the central hall is decorated with two rows of Ionic columns and, within frames painted on the walls, are depicted scenes from the Odyssey. A grand staircase, divided into two parts, leads to the first floor hall. Opening out of this hall are the three staterooms: the rotunda, a beautiful circular room used as a ballroom, the throne room on the left and the state dining room on the right. Behind these three rooms are two wings which were used by the High Commissioner as his private apartments, This is where the Museum of Asiatic Art is to be found today.

Collection of Christian Art. This collection is also housed in the Palace, in the same wing as that occupied by the Museum of Asiatic Art.

The Solomos Museum. This is situated in Corfu town, in the Mourayio area, in the house where Dionysios Solomos lived during the last years of his life.

Museum of the Fighters for Heptanesian Independence. This is housed in the restored building of the Ionian Parliament.

The **Municipal Gallery** possesses interesting old maps, portraits of the kings of Greece and paintings by some of the best-known Corfiot painters.

The **Antivouniotissa Monastery** houses a fine collection of paintings belonging to the Reading Society and interesting icons.

Left: Exhibits from the museum of Asiatic Art.

Right: Constantine Parthenis «Corfu landscape». (1917) Municipal Gallery.

CANONI - PONTIKONISSI

An easy, pleasant walk, a favourite of the older generations of Corfiots, is that which takes us around the **Canoni peninsula**, only 4 kms south of the town. Following Demokratias Avenue, along the coast, we pass the tomb of Menecrates. Here, when the Venetian fort of San Salvatore was demolished in 1843, the ancient cemetery of the Corcyreans was discovered . On our right is the suburb of **Garitsa**, and on our left the bay of the same name. Ahead lies the Anemo-mylos quarter, with the Byzantine church of SS. Jason and Sosipatros.

This same road which has brought us to Anenomylos continues, skirting the park of the palace of **Mon Repos**, built in 1831 to serve as the summer residence of the British High Commissioner, Sir Frederick Adam, and which later became the holiday home of the former royal family of Greece. Nearby are the ruins of the 5th-century basilica of Palaeopolis or St. Kerkyra, the oldest Christian monument of the island. An uphill road takes us to Analypsis hill, the acropolis of the ancient town, with scattered ruins of a 6th-century BC Doric temple. From here we can enjoy a magnificent view of the shores of Epirus across the strait. A path leads down from Analypsis hill to the sea, where the cool waters of the famous **Kardaki** spring flow from the open mouth of a Lion of St. Mark. According to local tradition, those who drink from this spring will never want to return home.

Canoni, one of the island's most idyllic spots.

Our walk ends at the lovely site of **Canoni**, at the southern tip of the Palaeopolis peninsula, and one of the island's main tourist attractions. It is still one of the most picturesque spots in Greece, despite the changes brought about by the rapid development of tourism in the area. It got its name from the cannon set up here by the French, which still reminds us today of the island's turbulent past. The landscape is idyllic, with the little island on which the *Vlachernes Monastery* is built in the foreground, and the "**Pontikonissi**" ("Mouse Island"), also known as "the island of Odysseus" further left. To get to the monastery, we descend some steps and cross the cement bridge connecting the islet to the mainland. From here one can take a caique to the charming "Mouse Island" - Corfu's trademark - with its little 13th-century church dedicated to Christ Pantocrator. According to legend, Pontikonissi is the Phaeacian ship that brought Odysseus back to his homeland, and was turned into stone by Poseidon. Canoni is linked to Perama opposite by a narrow bridge - for pedestrians and bicycles only - which crosses the Halikiopoulos lagoon.

→ Panoramic view from the islet on which stands the monastery of Vlacherna, or Vlacheraina, with picturesque Pontikonissi a short distance away.

NORTHERN CORFU

ITINERARY 1
Corfou
Kontokali, Gouvia
Kommeno, Dassia,
Ypsos, Pyrghi
Barbati, Nissaki
Kouloura, Aghios Stephanos
Kassiopi, Acharavi

ITINERARY 2
Pyrghi, Spartyllas, Episkepsi
Acharavi, Roda, Karousades
Sidari, Peroulades, Aghios Stephanos
Arillas, Aphionas, Aghios Georgios

Peroulades Sidari Rhoda Kassiopi
Ag. Stephanos Acharavi
Karousades Episkepsi Ag. Stephanos
Arillas Spartyllas Kouloura
Aphionas Καλάμι
Ag. Georghios Pyrghi Nissaki
Ypsos Barbati
Dassia
Kommeno
Gouvia
Kontokali
CORFU

Our tours of the beautiful island of Corfu will have its main town as starting point. the good road network makes the most important sites and some of the most characteristic villages easily accessible.

ITINERARY 1
Starting out from Corfu town in a northerly direction, we pass **Alykés** (4 kms from Corfu), a lively coastal settlement, well-equipped to welcome the tourist - as is all of the northeastern coast of the island. Opposite, at the entrance of the harbour of Corfu, lies the *islet of Vidos*, the ancient Ptychia. The road continues to **Kontokali**, with its high-quality tourist accommodation, and pleasure craft nestling inside its sheltered bay.

We then come to **Gouvia** (9 kms from town), which was once a Venetian naval base, and now has a NTO marina and is one of the most popular tourist resorts on the island. Opposite lies the islet of Lazaretto. A detour from Gouvia leads to the very interesting village of **Danilla**.

This is a faithful reproduction of a picturesque Corfiot village, with its houses, shops, narrow streets etc. Further north we come to Tzavro, and short detours to the east bring us to the villages of Limni, Kommeno and **Daphnila**, all popular with tourists and providing excellent hotel accommodation. Driving on, we come to the verdant coast of **Dassia** (13 kms from the town of Corfu), with the picturesque Polynesian straw huts of the Club Mediterranée. The entire area is particularly well developed from the point of view of tourism and offers many opportunities for beach and water sports and recreation. The road, still taking us northwards, deviates slightly from the coast, and passes through the charming village of Kato **Korakiana**.

Above: Gouvia.
Below: Dassia.

Above right: Ypsos.
Below right: Kouloura.

We come to the cosmopolitan resort of **Ypsos** ((15 kms from town), then to **Pyrghi** by the sea (both of these on the splendid beach known as the "Golden

Mile"), to Barbati, with its fine sand and rich vegetation coming all the way down to the water's edge, the beach of Glyfa, and Nissaki - a very popular beach with a charming cluster of houses built on the rocky shore. Now the road winds uphill and affords us a marvellous view of the coast and the *Pantocrator* mountain on the left. We pass outside Kentroma and continue onwards to **Gimari**, **Kalami** - a delightful little bay with a sandy beach - and **Kouloura**, a little fishing village.

The road then once more turns inland and, winding through beautiful scenery, comes to Cassiope (36 kms from town). A branch just after Kouloura brings us to the little cove of *Aghios Stephanos*, the closest point to the Albanian coast.

Cassiope, a picturesque little town with a harbour sheltering small craft, has been inhabited since antiquity, and in Roman times was a flourishing city, with an important port, a theatre, and a temple dedicated to Cassius Zeus, from which it derives its name. During its heyday, Cassiope was visited by the Roman orator Cicero and the emperor Nero, who played the lyre and sang before the altar of Zeus.

Almost nothing remains today of the prosperous Roman Cassiope. On the ruins of the ancient temple was built the church of Panaghia Cassopitra or Cassopitissa, destroyed by the Turks during their siege of the island and rebuilt by the Venetians in 1580, as is attested by the inscription in Latin on its northern gate. The castle on Cassiope hill, only ruins of which remain, was built by the Angevins and was one of the strongest fortresses of its time. Today, Cassiope has become a bustling tourist resort with no shortage of accommodation, tavernas, bars, discos etc.s

The coastal road continues to the northwest and passes by the little villages of Imerolia, Apraos, Magharika, Aghios Ilias, Pelekito, and Almyros, and ends up at **Acharavi** (10 kms from Cassiope), with its long sandy beach, on the

Above:
Acharavi

Below:
Panoramic view
of Cassiope.

northern coast of the island. From Aghios Ilias a secondary road leads to **Loutses** and
the traditional, listed village of **Ano
Peritheia**, with its stone houses and interesting churches, built high up on Pantocrator,
in a majestic mountain setting. This area is
of great archaeological interest, and com-
bines the charms of the mountain and the
sea, of tradition and modern comfort. At a
short distance lies the Antiniotis lagoon, a
wetland of great ecological importance.

ITINERARY 2

Up to **Pyrghi** we follow the same route as for itinerary 1. At this point, a branch to the left (2 kms) leads us to the village of **Aghios Markos**, with its two noteworthy churches - the *Pantocrator*, with frescoes dating from 1576, and *Aghios Merkourios*, whose frescoes date from 1075, and which is considered the most important Byzantine monument on the island after the church of St. Jason and Sosipatros. From the branch at Pyrghi we take the road which leads northwards, inland, towards some of the most picturesque mountain villages. At a distance of 19 kms from the town we meet the village of **Spartyllas**, on the slopes of Pantocrator (at an altitude of about 400 metres). This is a lovely village with a breathtaking view, abundant waters and lush verdure.

The road continues towards Sgourades, while a branch towards the right leads to the villages of **Strinylas** and **Petaleia**, with their characteristic stone houses, built on a small plateau of the Pantocrator. From here starts the ascent to the top of the Pantocrator mountain (914 m), which the Venetians knew as Monte San Salvatore. We can enjoy the panoramic view, and also visit the Pantocrator monastery, built in the mid-17th century on the site of an older ruined Angevin monastery. We continue along the main road from **Sgourades** towards **Episkepsi** (6 kms from the intersection), a charming traditional village, and further north we come to **Lazaratika** and **Acharavi**, near the northern coast of the island.

We drive on from the point where we stopped on our previous itinerary, in a westerly direction, along the northern coast of the island. We come upon the fine beaches of Rhoda (41 kms northwest of the town of Corfu), **Astrakeri**, and **Ai-Yiannis**. Outside Rhoda a branch of the road leads to the picturesque inland villages of **Sfakera**, **Platonas**, **Nymphes**, **Episkopi**, **Aghioi Doiloi** and **Choroespikopoi**.

The main road, after **Rhoda**, deviates slightly from the coast and passes through **Karousades**, a small town with attractive houses. We continue westwards towards Sidari, a tourist resort offering many amenities, situated on an open bay with a lovely sandy beach. In the area, traces of the island's first settlement, dating to the Neolithic age, have been found. From **Sidari**, caiques set out for the nearby islands of *Mathraki*, *Othonoi* and *Ereikoussa*.

Below: Roda.

Right: Peroulades

The characteristic porous rocks which the sea has sculpted into strange shapes, offer an impressive sight. Some of these rocks, rising out of the sea, form a sort of fjord, a natural canal, known as *"Canal d' Amour"*. A large part of it has been eroded and has crumbled, but the site has not lost its peculiar attraction.

The road continues to **Peroulades**, at the northwestern end of the island, and a side branch leads us to **Avliotes**. A smaller road leading southwards travels along the northwestern coast of the island, towards **Aghia Pelaghia**, **Aghios Stephanos**, on a small cape with a lighthouse, **Arillas**, with its lovely sandy beach 2,500 m long, enclosed by small peninsulas on either side. Before us lie the small islands of *Gravia*, *Diaplo* and *Mathraki*.

With their virgin sands, which one can visit in the summer months when excursions are organised. We then come to the attractive little harbour of **Aphionas**. In the area, which has recently experienced the development of tourism, there are ruins of ancient walls.

Deep within the bay of **Aghios Georgios** lie the settlements of **Agrilia** and **Aghios Georgios ton Pagon**, with olive and cypress trees growing almost to the edge of its marvellous beach.

Below: Canal d'Amour.

Right:
Aghios Stephanos
Arillas
Aghios Georgios
ton Pagon.

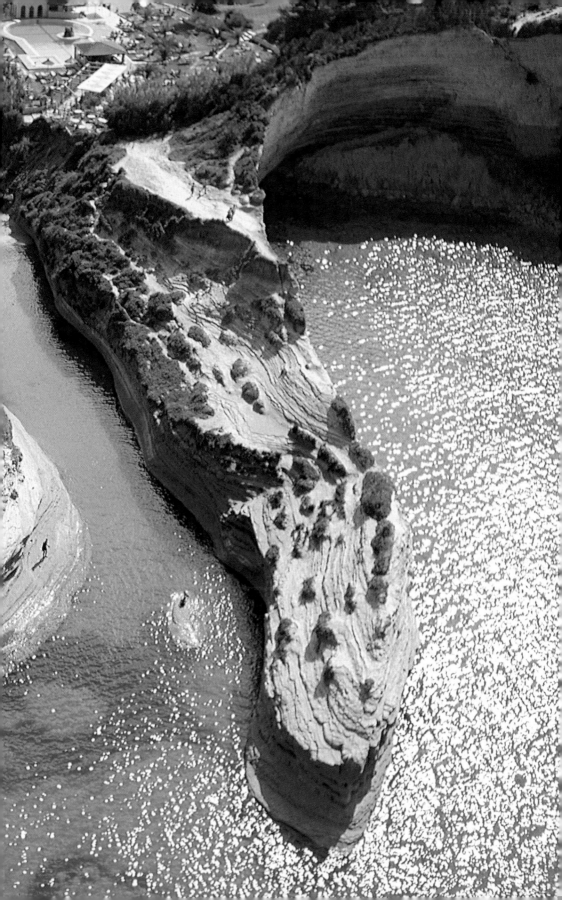

CENTRAL CORFU

ITINERARY 1

Corfou , Tzavros,
Aghios Vasilios,
Ano Korakiana
Skripero, Doukades,
Liappades, Lakones
Angelokastro
Paleokastritsa

ITINERARY 2

Kerkyra, Potamos, Giannades
Livadi Ropa
Ermones, Glyfada, Pelekas

ITINERARY 1

We take the same route as in Itineraries 1 and 2 up to **Tzavro**. We now turn left
for Aghios Vasilios and Ano Korakiana, in a northwesterly direction. Ano Korakiana
(18 kms from Corfu town) is a picturesque village with many churches and a long tradition
in choral music. In the area of Pelekas is to be found the largest ceramics factory of the island . Besides the noteworthy churches of the village (St. James - Aghios Iakovos, the
Archangel Michael, the Prophet Elijah, St. George, St. Athanasius), with their beautiful frescoes, portable icons and carved icon screens, the folk art collection, housed in the neo-clas-
sical building of the Primary School is also worth a visit.
Continuing to the west, we encounter the attractive traditional village of **Skripero**, with its
marvellous view. A detour outside the village brings us to *Perasma tou Troumbeta*, from
where we have a panoramic view of the area. This small road continues northwards to Cho-
roepiskopoi, and southwestwards to **Aleimmatades, Vistona, Makrades** and Krini, genuine
little Corfiot villages perched on hills, here and there, in an idyllic setting.

After the branch for Troumbeta, the road winds southwestwards towards **Doukades**, **Gardelades** and ends up at **Liapades**, a quiet village off the tourist track. The coastal settlement of Gefyra on Liapades bay is situated directly opposite Paleokastritsa, by a sea that is crystal-clear.

After Doukades, the road forks out. One branch ends up at Paleokastritsa and the other brings us to Lakones, Makrades and Krini. **Lakones** is a characteristic Corfiot village, built on a slope covered with olive trees. Just outside the village, on a small plateau known as *Bella Vista* ("beautiful view"), the visitor can admire the beauty of Paleokastritsa's bays from above, and see the verdant hills mirrored in the transparent waters.

At a distance of 3 kms lies **Krini**, from where one can ascend to *Angelocastro*. This 13th-century Byzantine castle is perched on a sheer crag opposite Paleokastritsa. It was built by Michael Angelos, the first despot of Epirus, and is known as the "Fortress of the Angels", and as "Castel Sant'

Liapades

Angelo". In 1403, Genoese pirates besieged the castle, but were unable to take it, thanks to the excellence of its fortifications. It dominates the entire area, and from its ramparts there is a view all the way to Corfu town.

The end of this route is the famed site of **Paleokastritsa**, perhaps the most picturesque corner of the island. The coastal settlement lies at a distance of 25 kms northwest of Corfu town. It extends along six bays of unparalleled beauty *(Aghia Triada, Platakia, Alipa, Aghios Spyridon, Aghios Petros, Ambelaki)*.

The sheer rocks, the verdant hills, the caves, sandy coves, lush olive groves, and the fortified Byzantine monastery of Paleokastritsa make up a picture which words alone cannot describe, and which only Nature herself can create. Some archaeologists have identified the area of Paleokastritsa with the site of the palace of king Alcinous. They believe that the acropolis of the Homeric town was situated where the monastery stands today, and that this was also where the meeting of Odysseus and Nausicaa took place.

The *monastery of the Holy Virgin of Paleokastritsa*, inhabited by monks, was founded in 1228. The present-day building complex, which includes the church, the cells and the spacious courtyard with its volta, was erected in the 18th century. There is a small but interesting collection of portable Byzantine and post-Byzantine icons, vestments, sacred books and liturgical vessels. Opposite the monastery, in the sea, rises the "stone ship" - the rock known as Kolovri - which legend identifies with the ship which had carried Odysseus home to Ithaca from the island of the Phaeacians, and which Poseidon's wrath turned to stone. According to another legend, this is the ship of an Algerian pirate, which was on its way to plunder the monastery, but which was turned to stone by the prayers of the abbot.

Naturally, Paleokastritsa is one of the most popular sites of the island for tourists, particularly as it has been a well-known cosmopolitan resort since the time of British rule. It offers every amenity, welcoming visitors in modern hotel complexes and other high quality accommodation, and offering them a choice of a variety of sports, shopping and entertainment, in its many shops, restaurants, bars, discos.

Monastery of Paleokastritsa

→

General view of Paleokastritsa

ITINERARY 2

We leave the town and take a northwesterly direction, we pass the attractive traditional village of **Potamos** with its multicoloured houses, and continue towards the area known as Livadi tou Ropa or *Ropa valley*, one of the most fertile parts of the island. Here is situated Corfu's golf course.

Further south lies **Ermones** (16 kms), a small bay with a sandy beach between imposing rocks and wooded hills. According to one theory, this is where the legendary meeting of Odysseus with the Phaeacian princess Nausicaa took place. This was also the favourite beach of the poet Lorentzos Mavilis who, it is said, used

to seek inspiration here, when writing his sonnets. In this area traces of habitation have been found which have been dated to the Bronze Age. South of Ermones there are another two superb beaches: Myrtiotissa and Glyfada. **Myrtiotissa** is reached on foot from a branch in the road between Vatos and Pelekas. It owes its name to an icon of the Virgin which was found by a little shepherd girl among the myrtle bushes in the area. The monastery of the same name which stands on the site today, was built 700 years ago. Myrtiotissa is an isolated beach set in impressive scenery, among lush verdure, and with a sea which is marvellous for swimming.

Glyfada (16 kms southwest of the town) is a long sandy beach at the foot of the Pelekas mountain. This is one of the parts of the island which are particularly developed from the point of view of tourism, and it offers many choices of sports and recreation. As we return towards the town, we pass through the traditional village of **Pelekas** with its characteristic houses, painted in vivid colours. It is built on one of the most beautiful hills of Corfu (272 m) and the view from here is breathtaking,

Above: Sunset at Pelekas

Below: Kontoyialos

especially at sunset, when the visitor can admire the splendour of the changing colours as the sun sinks slowly into the sea. On a plateau on the hilltop there is a natural balcony, where the Kaiser, William II, used to come and admire the sunset, and which has given the site its name, "*the Kaiser's throne*". From here one has a view inland, all the way to the town of Corfu, towards the olive groves to the north and the endless blue of the Ionian Sea. 2 kms from Pelekas lies the wonderful beach of **Kontoyialos**, a sandy inlet framed by verdant hills.

Right: Ermones and Glyfada.

From Pelekas we can return to Corfu town along a different route, and pass by the villages of **Aghia Triada, Kombitsi, Aghios Vlassis and Alepou**.

SOUTHERN CORFU

ITINERARY 1
Kerkyra, Kanali
Kastellanoi
Sinarades
Aghios Gordis, Garouna
Aghios Mathaios, Gardiki
Aghioi Deka, Kynopiastes

ITINERARY 2
Achilleion, Benitses
Aghios Ioannis Peristeron
Μοραΐτικα, Messoghi
Koryssia Lake
Argyrades, Lefkimi, Kavos

KERKYPA

Kanali
Kastellanoi
Sinarades
Perama
Aghios Gordis
Achilleion
Garouna
Benitses
Aghios Ioannis
Pavliana
Aghios Mathaios
Moraitika
Gardiki
Messoghi
Koryssia Lake
Argyrades
Aghios Georghios
Lefkimmi
Kavos

ITINERARY 1
From the town of Corfu we take a southwesterly direction. We pass the branch for Kanali and continue further south to Viro, Kastellanoi, Sinarades (18 kms from Corfu town). Sinarades is an old Corfiot village. The 15th-century Venetian belfry of its church is of particular interest, as is also its historical and folk art museum, housed in a traditional home, which exhibits items belonging to the rural households of the area. The road continues southwards, along the western coast. A small winding branch leads us through well-tended olive groves, planted on terraces descending all the way down to the sea, and the beach of Ai-Gordis. The view, as we drive downwards, is magnificent. The golden sands, together with the vivid blue of the sea and the dark green hues of the hills form a beautiful picture. On the left side of the bay a conical rock, the Ortholithi, rises sharply from the sea. Ai-Gordis

The entrance of the byzantine castle Gardiki.

is one of the most popular tourist resorts of the island, and offers ample accommodation, tavernas, bars etc. Four kilometres to the northeast is the site of *Aerostato*, a sheer rock from which there is a panoramic view.

The road turns inland and continues southwards towards Garouna, a village actually consisting of two separate settlements - those of Ano and Kato Garouna - built amphitheatrically on opposite hills. The village retains its vernacular architectural style, with its arches, volta, stone stairways, its traditional skills in stone carving and its local fêtes. The belfry of the church of St. Nicholas, carved by the able hands of local artisans, is an example of the traditional stonework. Further to the south lies another pair of "twin" communities: **Ano** and **Kato Pavliana** (20 kms from Corfu town). They too are traditional villages in a verdant setting, with a superb view.

The road continues southwards to Aghios Matthaios, a large inland village, 22.5 kms from Corfu town, built amphitheatrically at the foot of Mathios mountain, on a luxuriantly green hill, which also offers a beautiful view. On a slope of the same mountain stands the *monastery of Christ Pantocrator* (mid-14th century), and not far is a cave dating from Palaeolithic times. A detour, south of **Aghios Matthaios**, takes us to the ruins of the walls of the Byzantine *castle of Gardiki*. This is an octagonal fortress, built on a low hill, with eight mighty towers and ancient architectural members set in the walls. It belongs to the 13th century. One kilometre further to the southeast of Aghios Matthaios stands the Byzantine church of Panaghia.

We return to the town of Corfu following a south to north direction, through attractive inland villages: Strongyli, Kornata, Makrata, Aghioi Deka, which have retained their local style and their traditions.

Aghioi Deka is built on the slopes of the mountain of the same name, among dense olive groves, and the view from here is enchanting. We continue further north and meet **Kynopiastes**, a large traditional village with several interesting houses which are examples of the local vernacular architecture. Our route takes us back again to the town of Corfu.

ACHILLEION

From the town we take a southwesterly route, passing through **Kanali** and continuing towards **Gastouri**. This is a picturesque village 11.5 kms from the town, built at a short distance from the sea.

2 kms east of the village, on a small hill, is built the recently renovated **Achilleion**, the palace of the Austrian empress Elizabeth, or "Sissy". The "melancholy empress", as her biographers have called her, retreated to Corfu after the death of her son Rudolph. She was already familiar with the beauties of the island from previous trips when, in 1890, she decided to build the palace. She entrusted the plans to two renowned Italian architects from Naples, who presented her with the completed building in 1892. Influenced as she was by the Iliad, she gave the palace the name "Achilleion", and resided there off and on until 1898, when she was assassinated in Geneva. In 1908 the palace was bought by the German emperor, Kaiser William II, until 1914. The Achilleion is a neoclassical building, extremely ornate and impressive, which seems out of place in the natural environment. On the ground floor, in a series of rooms decorated in Pompeian style, are preserved personal items and mementoes which had belonged to Elizabeth and to the Kaiser, as well as various paintings, furniture etc. To the right of the entrance, there is a room decorated with wall paintings which served as a chapel. On the balcony with its Ionian peristyle, on the second floor, there are several pieces of sculpture, among them the busts of ancient Greek philosophers, of Shakespeare, statues of the nine Muses, of the Graces.

The Austrian empress, Elisabeth.

"The Triumph of Achilles".
Fresco adorning a wall of the Achilleion.

The palace is set among beautiful gardens, with a wonderful view towards the Halikiopoulos lagoon, Canoni, Pontikonissi, Perama, Pantocrator, and the mountains of Epirus opposite.

The gardens are adorned with various statues, of which the most important is the *"Dying Achilles"*, a work by the German sculptor Herter.

Further down stands the eight-metre-high bronze statue of *"Achilles Triumphant"*, the work of the German sculptor Goetz, which is of a dubious artistic quality.

There are also statues of Lord Byron, of the famous hetaera Phryne, and of the empress Elizabeth herself.

As we once more come onto the coastal road which leads from **Perama** to Moraitika, we pass through **Benitses** (12 kms), a seaside village, and one of the most popular of the island. Here, on a privately-owned piece of land, were found ruins of Roman baths.

In the village there is a maritime museum with interesting exhibits from the Mediterranean and other seas. Further south lies **Aghios Ioannis Peristeron** with its beautiful beach, and 20 kms from the town we come to **Moraitika**, which is very popular with tourists and offers abundant accommodation.

**Left above:
Perama.**

**Left below:
Benitses,**

Below: Moraitika.

Mesonghi. The road continues along the coast towards the inviting beach of **Mesonghi**, and then deviates slightly from the coast towards the *Koryssia lagoon*.

We continue southwards to **Argyrades**, a genuine Corfiot village of some importance (33 kms from the town), with traditional architecture, narrow streets with arches.

Beautiful beaches nearby are **Aghios Georgios Argyradon**, on the western coast, and **Boukaris**, **Aghia Paraskevi** and **Petriti** on the eastern coast.

Further south we come to **Lefkimmi** (42 kms from the town), the largest town of southern Corfu. Here are several traditional villages, many vineyards producing the famed local wine and a picturesque canal which divides the town into two.

A branch leads us to Lefkimmi cape and to **Alykés**. The main road continues towards the small communities of **Potami**, **Melikia** and **Kavos** (47 kms. from the town), - the latter an attractive beach surrounded by olive groves and cypress trees.

Right above:
Aghios Georgios
Argyradon.

Not far to the south, near cape **Asprokavos**, in a lovely verdant setting, lies the small fortified monastery of *Panaghia Arkoudila*, from where the view is magnificent. Nearby are the villages of *Paleohori, Neohori, Dragotina* and *Spartera*.

Right below:
Kavos.

HOW TO GET THERE

By Air: Olympic Airways link Corfu to Athens and Thessaloniki. The airport is situated 3 kms south of the town. Another airline operating services from Athens to Corfu is SEEA. During the peak season there are many charter flights from various European cities to the island.
By Car Ferry: Corfu is linked to Patras, Igoumenitsa, Paxos, Sayiada (Epirus) and Italy. One can get to Patras by KTEL bus or by train. From Athens and Thessaloniki there are regular KTEL bus services to Igoumenitsa.

SPORTS - ENTERTAINMENT

Besides swimming in the marvellous sea which surrounds the island, one can enjoy all kinds of water sports on most of the organized beaches of Corfu. Almost all the big hotels provide the necessary facilities and equipment for water sports. Many of these hotels also have tennis courts, while riding, sailing and cricket enthusiasts will be afforded the possibility of indulging in their hobbies. At Gouvia there is a marina, operated by the National Tourist Organisation. There is a golf course at "Livadi tou Ropa", where the necessary equipment may be hired.
Those who enjoy night life will find themselves in their element in Corfu, one of the most cosmopolitan islands in Greece. In town and in all the tourist resorts and villages there are discos, pubs, cafés, tavernas with floor shows. While those who seek that extra thrill can try their luck at the casino at Kanoni.

INTERESTING EVENTS

The most important events on Corfu are the religious festivals and village fêtes. First and foremost are the processions in honour of St. Spyridon, the island's patron saint. These take place four times a year: on Palm Sunday, on Good Saturday, on August 11 and on the first Sunday in November. On these occasions the embalmed body of the saint is carried through the town with ritual pomp and ceremony, accompanied by philharmonic bands from all over the island. The Corfiot carnival is celebrated in a particularly colourful way in the town and, on the last Sunday of carnival, there is a parade of floats to the musical accompaniment, again, of local philharmonic bands, after which King Carnival is set alight and burnt.
Most impressive are the religious ceremonies of Holy Week, which reach their climax on Easter Sunday. A picturesque local custom is the breaking of clay pots and vessels which are tossed out of windows and from the balconies of the town on the morning of Good Saturday. On

May 21, Corfu celebrates the union of the Ionian Islands with Greece. In summer there is a cricket festival with the participation of British teams. In summer, also, there are concerts given by the two municipal orchestras and the three philharmonic bands. In September, the Corfu Festival takes place, with performances of ballet, opera, theatre and concerts, with the participation of Greek and foreign artists and companies. Folk dance performances are held in the Old Fortress, during the summer months.

Many genuine traditional country fêtes, linked to religious festivals take place in many villages of the island. Besides the religious ceremonies, these comprise traditional folk dances and music.

LOCAL SPECIALITIES

The culinary specialities of Corfu are famous. One must try the "sofrito" (small slices of fried veal in a savoury sauce with garlic), the "pastitsada" (thick macaroni with veal in tomato sauce) and the "bourdetto" (special fish - preferably scorpion fish or rockfish, or tope - cooked in an onion sauce with plenty of red pepper). And one should also taste the "mandolata" - the delicious Corfu nougat - the fragrant strawberry liqueur, the kumquat confections and the excellent Kerkyrean wines.

ACCOMMODATION

Corfu offers in abundance all types and categories of accommodation. There are luxury hotels and bungalows, as well as A-, B-, C- D- and E-class hotels, furnished flats, pensions, rented rooms and camping sites.

Useful telephone numbers	(26610)
Tourist police	**30.265**
National Tourist Organisation (EOT)	**37.639, 37.520**
Port Authority	**32.655**
Municipality	**38.553**
General State Hospital	**45.811/5**
Corfu Hotel Association	**36.629**

HOTELS • HOTELS • HOTELS • HOTELS • HOTELS

NAME		TEL.
KERKYRA (26610)		
L	CORFU PALACE	39485-7
A	CAVALIERI	39041
B	ARCADION	37670-2
B	ASTRON	39505
B	BELLA VENEZIA	44290
C	ARCHONTIKO GARITSA	36950
C	ATLANTIS	35560
C	BRETAGNE	30724
C	DALIA	32341
C	HERMES	39321
C	IONION	39915
C	KONSTANTINOUPOLIS	48716-7
C	PHOENIX	42290
AG. GEORGIOS ARGYRADON (26620)		
B	BELLE VUE	51680-2
B	GOLDEN SANDS	51225
AGIOS GORDIOS (26610)		
A	AGIOS GORDIOS	53320-2
AGIOS IOANNIS PERISTERON (26610)		
A	CORFU VILLAGE	75031-3
A	MARBELLA BEACH	71183-7
B	ADONIS BEACH	72305
AGIOS IOANNIS TRIKLINON (26610)		
A	MARIDA	25542
AGIOS STEFANOS EPISKEPSIS (26630)		
B	APTS.BLUE BAY	63913
B	BLUE BAY APTS	63991
AHARAVI (26630)		
A	BASILIA HOTEL APTS	63968-9
A	CENTURY RESORT	63401-4
A	FILORIAN	63107
A	GELINA VILLAGE HOTEL & RESORT	64000-7
A	ST. GEORGE'S BAY COUNTRY CLUB	63203
B	AHARAVI BEACH	63460
B	BEIS BEACH	63913
B	DANDOLO	63557-8
B	IONIAN PRINCESS	63110

NAME		TEL.
ALIKES (26610)		
A	LOUIS KERKYRA GOLF	31785-9
B	SUNSET	31203
ANEMOMYLOS (26610)		
B	ARION	37950-1
B	PALACE MON REPOS	32783-5
ARMENADES (26630)		
B	OREA ELENI	96201-3
BARBATI (26630)		
B	ALEXIOU	91383
B	PANTOKRATOR	91005-7
BENITSES (26610)		
A	ODYSSEY APTS	71221-3
A	REGENCY	71211-8
A	SAN STEFANO	71112-8
B	ACHILLEUS	72425
B	BELVEDERE	72442
B	HESPERIDES	71211-8
B	POTAMAKI	71140
DAFNILA (26610)		
A	EVA PALACE	91237
A	GRECOTEL DAFNILA BAY	90230-4
B	NEFELI	91033
DASSIA (26610)		
A	CORFU CHANDRIS	97100-4
A	DASSIA CHANDRIS	97100-4
A	ELAEA BEACH	93490-3
A	IPSOS	80200
A	MAGNA GRAECIA PALACE	93053
B	EKATERINI	93350
B	LIVADI NAFSIKAS	97111-2
B	PALOMA BLANCA	93575
ERMONES (26610)		
A b.	ERMONES BEACH	94241-3
B	FILOXENIA	94660
GASTOURI (26610)		
B	BINZAN INN	56081
B	MONTANIOLA	56205

NAME		TEL.
GLIFADA (26610)		
A	LOUIS GRAND HOTEL GLYFADA CORFU	94140-5
B	GLYFADA BEACH	94257
GOUVIA (26610)		
A	DEMBONOS	91755
A	LOUIS CORCYRA BEACH	90196-8
B	MOLFETTA BEACH	91915-8
B	PARADISSOS	91001-2
B	PARK	91347
HLOMOS LEFKIMMIS (26620)		
A	CORFU BEACH PLAZA-RESORT	51717
IPSOS (26610)		
B	SUNRISE	93414
B	YPSOS BEACH	93232
KANONI (26610)		
L	CORFU HOLIDAY PALACE	36540
A	ARITI	33885-8
A	CORFU DIVANI PALACE	38996-8
KAROUSSADES (26630)		
A	REVEKKA VILLAGE	
B	CORFU MIRABEL	31310
KASSIOPI (26610)		
A	FROSSYNI'S GARDENS	81258
A	POSEIDON	81439
B	BALARI	81440
KATO KORAKIANA (26610)		
B	MISTRAL	93511
B	PALMA BEACH	93941-2
B	VICTORIA HILL	93994
KAVOS LEFKIMMIS (26620)		
B	CORFU ACRODILON	61362
B	SAINT MARINA	61345-6
KOMENO (26610)		
L	GRECOTEL CORFU	91490
A	KERKYRA CLUB MARINA	91504-5
A	RADOVAS	91218

NAME		TEL.
KONTOGIALOS SINARADON (26610)		
A	PELEKAS BEACH	95151-2
KONTOKALI (26610)		
L	KONTOKALI BAY	99000-2
A	INTERMEZZO APTS	91338
A	PRIFTIS HOUSE	91263
LIAPADES (26630)		
A	ELLY BEACH	41455
LOUTSES (26630)		
B	APRAOS BAY HOTEL	98004
MESSONGI (26610)		
A	APOLLON PALACE	75433
A	ARMONIA	75433
A	CHRISTINA	55294
B	GEMINI I	75211-2
MOLOS LEFKIMIS (26620)		
A	ATTIKA	334
MORAITIKA (26610)		
L	MIRAMARE BEACH	75224
A	DAISY	75343
A	DELFINIA	76230-3
B	ALBATROS	75315-7
B	ALKYONIS	75201
B	CAPODISTRIAS	75319
B	DELFINAKIA I	76320-3
B	DELFINAKIA II	75451-2
B	MESSONGHI BEACH	76684-6
NISSAKI (26630)		
L	ILIOS	22281-3
A	NISSAKI BEACH	91232-5
PALEOKASTRITSA (26630)		
A	AKROTIRI BEACH	41237
A	FOUNDANA VILLES	22532
B	PALEOKASTRITSA	41207
PARAMONAS (26630)		
B	PARAMONAS	76595-6

NAME		TEL.
PELEKAS (26610)		
A	KANTRY CLUB	33867
A	LEVANT	94230
PERAMA GASTOURIOU (26630)		
A	ALEXANDROS	36855-7
B	AEOLOS BEACH	33132-6
B	AKTI	36868
B	OASIS	38190
PERITHIA (26630)		
B	SAINT SPYRIDON BAY	98394
PERIVOLI LEFKIMMIS (26620)		
B	NAOS	22186
PEROULADES (26630)		
A	VILLA DE LOULIA	95394
PIRGI (26610)		
A	ANNA-LIZA	93438
B	AGHIOS NIKOLAOS	93883
B	GHIANNIS	93176
B	MARILENA	93891-4
RODA (26630)		
A	RODA BEACH	64181-5
B	IRINI VOURGIDIS	63586-7
B	PIGASSOS	63400
RODA SFAKERON (26630)		
B	CORAL	63490
SIDARI (26630)		
B	MONIKA	
SINARADES (26610)		
A	YALISKARI PALACE	54401-2
TSAKI (26610)		
B	BELLOS BEACH	72266
TZAVROS (26610)		
B	IONIAN ARCHES	91650
VASSILATIKA (26620)		
B	REGINA 52	132-4

ORGANIZED CAMPING SITES

NAME	LOCALITY	TEL.	NAME	LOCALITY	TEL.	NAME	LOCALITY	TEL.
AGIOS MATHEOS	Halikountas	26610-75069	IPSOS IDEAL	Ipsos	26610-93243	PALEOKASTRITSA	Paleokastritsa	26630-41104
CORFU	Ipsos	26610-93246	KARDA BEACH	Dasia	26610-93595	PARADISE	Pyrgi	26610-93282
DIONYSUS	Kato Korakiana	26610-91417	KAROUSADES	Karousades	26630-31415	RODA BEACH	Roda	26630-63120
DOLPHIN	Karoussades	26630-31522	KONTOKALI BEACH INTERNATIONAL		26610-91170	SAN GEORGE	Kavadades	26630-51012
IPPOKAMBOS	Messogi	26610-75364	KORMARI	Kormari, Dasia	26610-93587	VATOS	Vatos, Pelekas	26610-94505

PRODUCTION-PRINTING-BINDING : **PERGAMOS PRINTING AND PUBLISHING S.A.**